MW01062486

RENA RHINOCEROS

Rena the Rhinoceros

"I Am Reading Latin Stories" Series

Book Four

This is one of a series of Latin books developed for ages 5–8. Other books include

Ursus et Porcus: The Bear and the Pig **(Book One)**
Octavus Octopus: Octavus the Octopus **(Book Two)**
Taurus Rex: King Bull **(Book Three)**

Check www.bolchazy.com for more information.
Recordings of these books also will be on the website.

Why learn Latin?

A short answer is that Latin

- develops a person's English
- provides a solid foundation for the acquisition of other languages
- connects us with the cultures of 57 nations on 4 continents
- provides us with cultural roots and a sense of identity
- enhances our career choices

Latin vocabulary forms the basis of 60% of the words in the English language, and it also forms the roots of the Spanish, French, and Italian languages. The very act of learning Latin serves to increase the mind's analytic processes, and an exposure to the Roman world constitutes a journey back to the roots of our own Western heritage. It's never too early to start learning Latin.

An "I Am Reading Latin Stories" Book

RENA RHINOCEROS

Rena the Rhinoceros

By Rose Williams

Illustrated By

James Hillyer Estes

Bolchazy-Carducci Publishers, Inc.
Mundelein, Illinois USA

General Editor: Marie Bolchazy
Latin Editor: John Traupman
Cover Design & Layout: Adam Phillip Velez
Illustrations: James Hillyer Estes

Rena Rhinoceros
Rena the Rhinoceros

Rose Williams

Bolchazy-Carducci Publishers, Inc.
1570 Baskin Road
Mundelein, Illinois 60060
www.bolchazy.com

Printed in the United States of America
2019
by Publishers' Graphics

978-0-86516-699-8

Library of Congress Cataloging-in-Publication Data

Williams, Rose, 1937-
  Rena Rhinoceros / by Rose Williams ; illustrated by James Hillyer Estes.
    p. cm. -- (I am reading Latin stories series)
  ISBN 978-0-86516-699-8 (pbk. : alk. paper) 1. Latin language--Readers--Juvenile literature. [1. Latin language--Readers.] I. Estes, James Hillyer. II. Title.

PA2095.W565 2008
871'.01--dc22

                                                      2008024325

Rēna est animal īnfāns. Rēna est rhīnocerōs.

1

ingēns = giant, huge
cāna = gray
cornū = horn

Māter Rhīnocerōs est ingēns. Māter
Rhīnocerōs est cāna colōre. Māter
Rhīnocerōs cornū magnum in nasō habet.

Pellis = skin
Crassa = thick

"Māter," dīcit Rēna, "tū es cāna colōre; ego sum
cāna colōre. Pellis tua est crassa; pellis mea
est crassa. Sed tū cornū in nāsō habēs. Quid
sum?"

"Tū es rhīnocerōs, cāra," dīcit māter.

"Sī rhīnocerōs sum, cūr cornū in nāsō nōn
habeō?"

3

"Tū es īnfāns, cāra. Fortasse cornū nōn habēs quod tū es parva."

dēsīderō : want

"Īnfāns sum, sed cornū dēsīderō. Rhīnocerōs
cornū in nāsō habēre dēbet."

grāmine=grass

Rēna Rhīnocerōs in grāmine ambulat.
"Rhīnocerōs nōn sum. Cornū in nāsō nōn
habeō. Fortasse elephantus sum."

Pellem: skin
Proboscidem: trunck

Rēna parvum elephantum spectat. Elephantus est cānus colōre. Elephantus pellem crassam habet. Elephantus cornū in nāsō nōn habet, sed elephantus proboscidem habet.

"Nōn sum elephantus," dīcit Rēna. "Fortasse hippopotamus sum."

Rēna parvum hippopotamum spectat.
Hippopotamus est cānus colōre.
Hippopotamus pellem crassam habet. Sed
hippopotamus nāsum lātum et saetās habet.

"Nōn sum hippopotamus," dīcit Rēna. "Nōn sum elephantus.
Ō, quid sum? Quid sum?"

Māter, quae ambulat post Rēnam, dīcit, "Rēna, spectā in aquam. Spectā tē et mē."

"Esne tū similis mihi? Esne cāna colōre? Estne pellis tua crassa? Estne nāsus tuus similis nāsō meō?"

"Sed cornū in nāsō nōn habeō," dīcit Rēna.

"Cornū in nāsō habēbis cum eris magna. Nunc est tempus crēscere et discere. Crēsce et disce nunc, et in tempore eris magna et bona rhīnocerōs."

"Exspectābō, Māter," dīcit Rēna. "Dēsīderō crēscere et discere. Grātiās tibi agō. Ego tē amō, Māter."

13

Tūber: Small bump, lump

Rēna in aquam iterum spectat. "Tūber in nāsō
   meō spectō!
Mox cornū in nāsō habēbō!" Rēna clāmat.

Dēsignā verbum corrēctum.

1. Rēna est animal _īnfāns_ .

   a. fortis b. īnfāns c. ingēns

2. Māter Rhīnocerōs est _cāna_ colōre.

   a. cāna b. fortis c. īnfāns

3. Māter Rhīnocerōs _cornū_ magnum in nāsō habet.

   a. pēdem b. grāmen c. cornū

4. Rēna est cāna _____ .

   a. colōre b. magnitūdine c. pede

5. Rēna in nāsō _____ dēsīderat.

   a. pedem b. grāmen c. cornū

6. Elephantus _____ habet.

   a. proboscidem b. cornū c. aquam

7. Hippopotamus nāsum lātum et _____ habet.

   a. saetās b. cornū c. māter

8. Māter dīcit, "Rēna, spectā in _____ .

   a. grāmen b. aquam c. silvam

9. Māter dīcit, "Nunc est tempus _____ .

   a. ambulāre et spectāre b. crēscere et discere c. spectāre et dīcere

Translation

Rena is a baby animal. Rena is a rhinoceros.

The mother rhinoceros is huge. The mother rhinoceros is grey in color. The mother rhinoceros has a large horn on the nose.

"Mother," says Rena, "you are grey in color; I am grey in color. Your skin is thick; my skin is thick. But you have a horn on the nose. I do not have a horn on the nose. What am I?"

"You are a rhinoceros, dear," says mother.

"If I am a rhinoceros, why do I not have a horn on the nose?"

"You are a baby, dear. Perhaps you do not have a horn because you are small."

"I am a baby, but I want a horn. A rhinoceros ought to have a horn on the nose."

Rena Rhinoceros walks in the grass. "I am not a rhinoceros. I do not have a horn on the nose. Perhaps I am an elephant."

Rena sees a small elephant. The elephant is grey in color. The elephant has thick skin. The elephant does not have a horn on the nose, but the elephant has a trunk.

"I am not an elephant," says Rena. "Perhaps I am a hippopotamus."

Rena sees a small hippopotamus. The hippopotamus is grey in color. The hippopotamus has thick skin. But the hippopotamus has a wide nose and whiskers.

"I am not a hippopotamus," says Rena. "I am not an elephant. O what am I? What am I?"

The mother, who is walking behind Rena, says, "Rena, look in the water. Look at you and me."

"Are you like me? Are you grey in color? Is your skin thick? Is your nose like my nose?"

"But I don't have a horn on the nose," says Rena.

"You will have a horn on the nose when you are large. Now is the time to grow and to learn. Grow and learn now, and in time you will be a big and good rhinoceros."

"I will wait, Mother," says Rena. "I want to grow and to learn. Thank you. I love you, Mother."

Rena looks in the water again. "I see a bump on my nose! Soon I will have a horn on the nose!" Rena shouts.

Dēsignā verbum corrēctum answers.
(Choose the correct word)

1. B   2. A   3. C   4. A   5. C

6. A   7. A   8. B   9. B

Pronunciation Guide

Latin words generally have no silent letters. You can break the words up into pieces and pronounce them one piece at a time until you learn them. A slanting stroke — ' — follows the part of the word to be accented.

Here is a simple guide to how vowels sound. The long vowels are usually pronounced twice as long as the short; they sound like the vowels in these English words:

Long		Short	
ā as in father	Māter	*a* as the first sound in aha	am' bu lat
ē as in they	Rē' na	*e* as in bet	est
ī as in machine	īn' fāns	*i* as in bit	in
ō as in vote	nōn	*o* as in omit	hip po pot' amus
ū as in rule	tū	*u* as in but	sum

Diphthong (two vowels pronounced very quickly together)
ae -ah-ē (aisle) sae' tās

Consonants
Most are the same as English. Here are the notable exceptions.
c is always hard as in cake	ca' ra
g is always hard as in get	in' gēns
s is always hissed; never *z*	es
v is pronounced *w*	par' va

A Note About Pronunciation

In this story there are some long words which are names of animals. The ancient people often named animals because of their appearance, so "rhīnocerōs" means "nose horn," and "hippopotamus" means "river horse." Long words like these are divided into syllables. If the next to the last syllable has a long mark over the vowel or another reason for being long, it is stressed. If the next to last syllable does not have a reason for being long, the third from the last is stressed. Therefore "hip po po' ta mus" is the correct pronunciation. Words such as "rhīnocerōs" and "elephantus," which have the letter 'h' after another consonant, are pronounced without the 'h'. These animals are pronounced "rī no' ce rōs" and "e le pan' tus."

Glossary

am′bu lō, am′bu lā′re   to walk   AMBLE, AMBULATORY
a′mō, a mā′re   to love   AMANDA
a′ni mal, a ni mā′lis   *n.* animal   ANIMAL
a′qua, a′quae   *f.* water   AQUATIC
bo′nus, bo′na, bo′num   good   BON-BON
cā′nus, cā′na, cā′num   grey
cā′rus, cā′ra, cā′rum   dear   CHARITY
crē′sco, crē′sce re   to grow   INCREASE
clā′mō, clā′mā′re   to shout   EXCLAIM
co′lor, co lōr′is   *m.* color   COLOR
cornū, cornūs   *n.* horn   CORN
cras′sus, cras′sa, cras′sum   thick   CRASS
cum   when (takes a future verb)
cūr   why
dē sī′de rō, dē sī de rā′re   to want   DESIRE
dē′be ō, dē bē′re   to owe, ought   DEBT
dī′cō, dī′ce re   to say   DICTATE
di′scō, di′sce re   to learn   DISCIPLE
ego   I   EGOIST
e le phan′tus, e le phan′tī   *m.* elephant   ELEPHANT
eris   you will be
et   and
ex spec′tō, ex spec′ tā′re   to wait   EXPECT
for tas′se   maybe
grā′men, grā′min is   *n.* grass
grā′ti ās ti′bi a′gō   I thank you   GRATITUDE
ha′be ō, ha bē′re   to have   HABIT
hip po po′ta mus, hip po po′ta mī   *m./f.* hippopotamus
in   (with acc.) into, onto (with abl.) in, on
īn′fāns, īn fan′tis   *m./f.* baby   INFANT
in′gēns, in gen′tis   huge
i′te rum   again
lā′tus, lā′ta, lā′tum   wide   LATITUDE
mag′nus, mag′na, mag′num   big   MAGNIFICENT
mā′ter, mā′tris   *f.* mother   MATERNAL
mē   me (direct object)
me′us, me′a, me′um   my
mi′hi   to me
mox   soon

nā'sus, nāsī   *m.* nose   NASAL
-ne   (question mark)
nōn   not
nunc   now
par'vus, par'va, par'vum   small
pel'lis, pel'lis   *f.* skin
pro bos'cis, pro bos'ci dis   *f.* trunk
post   (with acc.) behind
quae   who
quid   what?
quod   because
rhī no'ce rōs , rhī no ce rō'tis   *m./f.* rhinoceros
sae'ta, sae'tae   *f.* whisker
sed   but
sī   if
si'mi lis, si'mi le   like   SIMILE
spec'tō, spec tā're   to look (at)   SPECTACLE
tē   you (direct object)
tem'pus, tem'po ris   *n.* time   TEMPORAL
tū   you (subject)
tū'ber, tū'be ris   *n.* bump, lump   TUBER
tu'us, tu'a, tu'um   your

Irregular Verb **esse** "to be"

sum - I am	**sumus** - we are
es - you are	**estis** - you (plural) are
est - he, she, it is	**sunt** - they are

Present Tense of Verb **habeō**

habeō - I have	**habēmus** - we have
habēs - you have	**habētis** - you (plural) have
habet - he, she, it has	**habent** - they have

Future Tense of **habeō**

habēbō - I shall, will have	**habēbimus** - we shall, will have
habēbis - you will have	**habēbitis** - you (plural) will have
habēbit - he, she it, will have	**habēbunt** - they will have

Note About Latin Word Endings

In English the place of words in a thought or sentence is shown by the order in which the words come. The subject and words that go with it usually come first, the verb comes second, and the direct object and words that go with it come last. In Latin the place of words in a thought or sentence is shown by how the words are spelled.

Look at the forms of "**nāsus**" (nose):

> **Nāsus longus est.**   The nose is long.
> **Māter nāsum magnum habet.**   The mother has a big nose.

The subject of a sentence may end in various letters, but the direct objects in this story end in "**m**," "**s**," or "**ū**." A word following a little word called a preposition may end in "**ā**," "**ō**," "**ī**" or "**e**" if the preposition takes the ablative (abl.). In this story a word following a preposition which takes the accusative (acc.) ends in "**m**," "**s**" or "**ū**." You can see that the meaning of the preposition changes according to the accusative (acc.) word or the ablative (abl.) word which follows it.

Adjectives (words which tell about the nouns) usually end in "**s**" or "**um**" if the word is marked *m* (masculine) or *n* (neuter) in the glossary, and with "**a**," "**am**" or "**s**" if the word is marked *f* (feminine)in the glossary. In this story there is a special ablative noun which describes or explains an adjective. "**Colōre**" used after the word "**cāna**" means "in color." "**Cāna colōre**" means "grey in color."

Words such as "**rhīnocerōs**" and "**elephantus**" may refer to animals which are either male or female. The adjectives which go with them often show whether they are male or female; for example, "**Rhīnocerōs est magna et elephantus est parva.**"

Notice that the verb also changes. "**Spectāre**" means "to look (at)." "**Spectat**" means "he, she or it looks (at)." "**Spectā**" is the command "look (at)."

Look carefully at the verb charts given. You can see that the verb ending "**ō**" or "**m**" means "I." "**Habeō**" means "I have," "**habēs**" means "you have," and so on.

When the verb refers to something in the future, the letters "**b**," "**bi**" or "**bu**" may be added in the middle of the verb to represent "will." You do not say the word "he," "she," or "it" when there is a subject such as "**māter**" or "**Rēna**." The word "**tū**" for the subject "you" or the word "**ego**" for "I" may be used for extra emphasis or contrast.